Take
Great
Notes

Sara Miller McCune founded SAGE Publishing in 1965 to support the dissemination of usable knowledge and educate a global community. SAGE publishes more than 1000 journals and over 800 new books each year, spanning a wide range of subject areas. Our growing selection of library products includes archives, data, case studies and video. SAGE remains majority owned by our founder and after her lifetime will become owned by a charitable trust that secures the company's continued independence.

Los Angeles | London | New Delhi | Singapore | Washington DC | Melbourne

SUPER
QUICK
SKILLS

Take Great Notes

Mal Leicester
Denise Taylor

Los Angeles | London | New Delhi
Singapore | Washington DC | Melbourne

Los Angeles | London | New Delhi
Singapore | Washington DC | Melbourne

SAGE Publications Ltd
1 Oliver's Yard
55 City Road
London EC1Y 1SP

SAGE Publications Inc.
2455 Teller Road
Thousand Oaks, California 91320

SAGE Publications India Pvt Ltd
B 1/I 1 Mohan Cooperative Industrial Area
Mathura Road
New Delhi 110 044

SAGE Publications Asia-Pacific Pte Ltd
3 Church Street
#10-04 Samsung Hub
Singapore 049483

Editor: Jai Seaman
Editorial assistant: Lauren Jacobs
Production editor: Victoria Nicholas
Marketing manager: Catherine Slinn
Cover design: Shaun Mercier
Typeset by: C&M Digitals (P) Ltd, Chennai, India
Printed in the UK

Library of Congress Control Number: 2019933320

British Library Cataloguing in Publication data

A catalogue record for this book is available from
the British Library

ISBN 978-1-5264-8941-8

At SAGE we take sustainability seriously. Most of our products are printed in the UK using responsibly
sourced papers and boards. When we print overseas we ensure sustainable papers are used as measured
by the PREPS grading system. We undertake an annual audit to monitor our sustainability.

Contents

Everything in this book!

Section 1   Why should I take notes?

Notes help you to be a good student. An aide-mémoire for assignments and exam revision, they encourage active learning and become a manageable, concise, organized record of your studies.

Section 2   What are good notes like?

Good notes are clear, well organized, accurate, concise, accessible, and useful. In this book you will learn how to take and make notes and how to store them.

Section 3   How do I use digital technology to take notes?

Electronic devices are an everyday part of life. Digital methods of note-taking can help you to capture and retrieve information more easily and help you to be more organized.

Section 4   What is the outline method of note-taking

We now look at different note-taking methods, beginning with the outline method. This uses indents, headings, and subheadings to organize notes, highlighting the relative importance of aspects within the material.

Section 5   What is the Cornell method of note-taking

The Cornell is a popular page layout method. The page is easily divided, in advance, into sections. These encourage an organized record together with your own ideas and a summary.

Section 6   What is the charting method of note-taking

First you prepare a chart with the relevant columns and headings. Charts enable you to present statistical and factual data for easier assimilation of substantial information and for making comparisons.

Section 7   What are the visual methods of note-taking?

Visual note-taking methods use structures (mind maps and spider diagrams), images, and organizers or connectors to capture and present information graphically without being text heavy.

Section 8   What are the electronic methods of note-taking?

Electronic note-taking captures information using digital devices including laptops, tablets, mobile phones, audio, and video recorders. A variety of apps can be used on these devices to support note-taking.

Section 9   How do I take notes in a lecture?

Capturing concepts and ideas from lectures requires preparation and making good use of the tools and processes best suited to your learning preferences and the task at hand.

Section 10   How do I take notes on an article or book?

We show you how to take useful notes on an article or book. Starting from a clear understanding of the text, you must condense it while retaining the important elements.

Why should I take notes?

10 second summary

Note-taking is an essential academic skill. It will help you to learn and to remember, to pick out and organize key material, and to write better assignments and examination answers.

60 second summary

Notes help you to be a good student

In your assignments, you need to show what you have learned from your lectures, but how will you remember these without notes? You need to show you understand core themes and arguments. Notes are a record of these key points or ideas. They are also a record of your reading. Always keep details of the author, title, date, and publisher. These details will help you to produce accurate references. When you revise for your examinations, notes are an invaluable aide-mémoire. They can help you to revise effectively and efficiently. All the material you need for your revision is readily accessible and concise.

The advantages

1 Taking notes on your lectures and on the books and articles you read will be a huge help in writing a good assignment and in revising for your exams.

2 When you take notes you listen with more attention. You remain more focused and thus become an active learner.

Organize Arrange and form into a logical sequence.

3 Your notes provide a concise, organized record of your studies.

Academic Learned, theoretical, of the University. An academic is a university teacher.

4 You will develop the core academic skill of picking out the most essential points, the most important arguments, and the influential ideas.

Aide-mémoire Something to help you remember, a reminder.

5 Notes are an aide-mémoire containing all the key ideas from your studies.

Note-taking and note-making

The terms *note-taking* and *note-making* tend to be used interchangeably. We will use *note-taking* for your first draft notes, made as you listen or read. We will use *note-making* for your second draft notes, made when you redo your first draft, amending, pruning, and adding, to produce a better organized and clearer aide-mémoire.

A student told us

'I can't concentrate for long when I'm listening to a lecture or reading a book.'

No one can! Our minds wander. ['What shall I have for lunch?'] Taking notes will help you to stay focused. You are being an active not a passive learner.

Develop your own notable ideas

- Making notes will stimulate your own ideas and you will see links with other ideas. Make a note of these too (for example, in brackets or a different colour to show they are your own).

- Think critically as you redo your notes and as you read over them.

- Knowing what influential writers have said, together with having your own ideas about what they have said, will help you to get even better grades!

Don't drown! Notes are your lifebelt

Without notes you can get a bit lost in the sea of information and ideas. By taking notes you get anchored into your studies. Just as you can get absorbed in a good film or book, by taking notes you get drawn into your subject and thus get more control of it.

Notes help you to:

- remember your studies, especially the key ideas.

- write better assignments and do examination revision effectively.

- have your own organized and concise learning materials.

CHECK POINT Reviewing the value of note-taking

Without looking back at what you have read above, can you answer the following?

What are four advantages of note-taking?

....

....

....

What core academic skill will note-taking help you to develop?

....

....

....

How can notes help you to revise?

....

....

....

What is an 'active learner'?

....

....

....

ACTIVITY Remembering more by taking notes

Practise how to take notes as you go

1   Listen to the evening news. Do not take notes, but do notice how
    many items are included.

    Four hours later, how many of these can you remember? Jot down
    the items you can remember below.

    ....

    ....

    ....

    ....

    ....

2   On the same day the following week, listen to the evening news
    again. This time note down each item or news story (for example,
    1. New Brexit controversy; 2. Car crash on M1 kills two people and
    delays traffic for eight hours; etc.).

    ....

    ....

    ....

    ....

    ....

Four hours later, how many of these news items can you recall? Jot them down below.

....

....

....

....

....

'Don't forget. Make a Note!'

SECTION
TWO

What are good notes like?

10 second summary

Good notes are legible, unambiguous, concise, correct, relevant, and organized. They will be well taken by and suited to the note-taker. Above all, good notes will be useful and reader (student) friendly.

Good notes are your key to success

Good notes are the key to successful study. Correct, concise, and clear notes which contain all, but **only**, the important stuff are a useful tool for your assignments and your examination revision. Good, relevant notes help you to do better assignments without getting overwhelmed by too much material. They help you to do focused, relevant revision. Include your own ideas, perhaps in a different colour, ideas which will be stimulated by taking notes. Well-organized notes, which use headings and subheadings, will help you to understand the structure of your study material and well-stored notes will save you time.

Organize your notes

- Because you took your notes while you were reading or listening, they may not be as organized as they could be. Ideally, you should redo them, by hand or typing, as soon as possible after you made the original notes.

- Write headings for each new topic to give them a good shape. For long paragraphs you could use some subheadings.

- You can also use bullet points to organize your material or numbering with the most important points coming first.

- Check that all the important concepts and arguments have been included.

  Concept An idea, often a general or abstract idea.

- Assignment and exam assessors like to see that you have developed some of your own ideas. In your notes include your own ideas in brackets or use a different colour.

Abbreviations

Your notes will only be useful if they are easy to read and cover all the topics. You can use abbreviations to keep up with the speaker. Here are some commonly used abbreviations. You will find that you develop some of your own personal ones too.

Common abbreviations:

Plus	+	Information	info
Possibly	poss	Example	eg.
Less than	<	**My own:**	
More than	>	Knowledge	kn
Compared to	cf	Important	imp

A kind of summary

Good notes only contain the main points of lectures and books! They screen out irrelevant asides, long anecdotes, and multiple examples. They should help you to record and, later, revise and remember the key material. They are a kind of summary of your studies – keeping the important material and leaving out the rest. This will give you an overview of the topics you have covered in your course – don't worry if you don't capture every word.

Don't panic about the idea of doing a kind of summary. Simply leave out repetitions, irrelevant asides, jokes and stories, and more than one brief example illustrating a point. Also, do not use wasted words – those not needed for the sentence to make sense, e.g. *very* (see Activity: How to improve a note).

> **Summary** A shortened form of a piece giving only the main points.

Less is more! Be concise

- Notes are a short version of the original.

- An author or lecturer often begins a new paragraph or section with the essential idea or topic for that paragraph or section. Develop the skill of picking out these key things, the bones of the piece.

- Your notes should not contain examples or anecdotes unless they are necessary for understanding the point being made.

A student told us

'People always misunderstand what I write. How can I make it clearer?'

Write in short, simple sentences using words that you are sure you understand correctly. Check for anything that could be read in two ways and remove the ambiguity!

A recap

To provide accurate references to a book or paper you must include the author, title, date of publication, publisher and place of publication. These details must, of course, all be correct.

Your notes must be legible. In other words, if handwritten the writing must be clear and if typed the typing must be neat. Avoid long sentences. Subdivide the longer paragraphs.

When a sentence or word could mean two different things, change the wording so that the meaning you intend is clear.

Put your own ideas in brackets or use a different colour so that you will easily recognize material of your own that you have added.

Well-organized notes will use headings, subheadings in long paragraphs, and bullet points for a list of tips, arguments, advantages, or suggestions, for example. There is advice below about storing your notes.

Reviewing your notes

Are your references accurate? ❏

Are your notes easy to read? ❏

Are your notes unambiguous? ❏

Have you included your own ideas and comments and differentiated these so it is clear that they are yours? ❏

Have you deleted wasted words? ❏

Do your notes contain any unnecessary material? ❏

Are your notes well organized? ❏

Be good: Storing your notes

1 If you use a notebook write the name of the subject at the front with headings for each separate set of notes. Keep your notebook in a safe place.

2 If you use loose paper, keep it in a folder. Label the folder. Number the pages.

3 If you save your notes electronically, organize them in folders with clear file names and make sure you do a regular back-up.

ACTIVITY How to improve a note

Rewrite the following note about poor handwriting. Remove irrelevances and wasted words and give the note some shape. Compare your remade note with the good example we provide on the next page.

You may find it really difficult to read your own writing. What can you do about this? You really need to read your notes as soon as you possibly can so that you are much more likely to be able to work out what you wrote. I know that when I make notes my handwriting becomes a scrawl! When you have read your notes have you considered that it might be better to type them all and this gives you a chance, as you type, to remember to make what you wrote unambiguous and to put in headings and bullet points. If something that is really useful and relevant occurs to you as you type, you could put it in brackets or type it in red or green. Some people say that you cannot change your handwriting but in fact practice can really improve it. You could practice improving your handwriting skills.

Example of an improved note

Poor handwriting

You may find it difficult to read your own writing. It helps to redo notes as soon as possible.

- It may be better to type them.

- Clarify any ambiguities.

- Organize the material (headings, bullet points, etc.).

- Put your own ideas in brackets or use a different colour.

Practice

You could practise improving your handwriting skills.

'Good students take good notes.'

How do I use digital technology to take notes?

10 second summary

Electronic devices are an everyday part of life. Digital methods of note-taking can help you to capture and retrieve information more easily and help you to be more organized.

Using digital technology to take notes

The digital age is transforming learning. Most universities now use the Internet and online platforms for assigning tasks, uploading reading lists and other resources you might need, as well as submitting your assignments online for your tutors to mark. You are now likely to receive your marks and grades electronically.

Most also offer courses that are delivered online. These can be whole courses as part of a distance learning programme or online courses that form part of your overall degree. Some universities even offer degree courses that are delivered wholly online.

In fact, it seems that everything about universities is entering the digital age. Internet access is widely available on campus, lecture theatres are equipped with state of the art equipment, and you will have access to a vast store of online books, papers, and articles accessible via your online library pass.

Upgrade your note-taking to digital

- Digital note-taking is more than word processing on a laptop or tablet. You can use a wide range of apps (applications) and devices to capture part or even all of the lectures you attend.

  > **Digital** methods of recording or storing information electronically.

- You can create, organize, and even share revision notes that are accessible across multiple devices.

  > **App** An application that can be downloaded to a mobile device or computer.

- You can capture and organize your concepts, ideas, and research for essay writing.

- You can create digital templates for note-taking which will help your productivity.

- You can import PDFs, images, and other files into your digital notes and annotate these.

- Audio and video recording devices and apps allow you to capture all of the lecture. You can then watch or listen to the recordings afterwards to strengthen your notes and your learning.

- Some universities video record all their lectures and make these available to students online.

Do you already have the tools?

These days, most students already have a number of digital tools at their disposal. You will have access to the Internet via your laptop, mobile phone, or tablet. Your university will also provide you with digital tools and platforms. Do a quick inventory of what is already available to you.

Does your phone or tablet have good recording facilities for video and audio recording? What apps do you already have that you can use? Do you have a tablet such as iPad Pro, Microsoft Surface Pro, or Samsung Galaxy Tab, which will allow you to take handwritten digital notes? You may already be a fan of Microsoft OneNote, Evernote, or GoodNotes. Or you may use another app or program that you find useful.

Do your research, find some options

If you don't already have the tools, apps, and programmes, it's easy to find them. The world of learning online is increasing rapidly, and this includes lots of video tutorials, online courses on sites such as Udemy (www.udemy.com) and FutureLearn (www.futurelearn.com), blogs, and web pages on studying. Simply typing in 'taking great notes' into Google or YouTube searches will bring you a vast array of information. Although this might at first seem daunting, you will quickly learn what appeals to you, and there are blogs that will help you to make comparisons. YouTube has lots of video tutorials that teach you about the benefits of using apps and programs such as Microsoft OneNote, Goodnotes, and Evernote. All of these offer great note-taking facilities, and most of these tools have a level that you can access for free or at low cost.

What should you choose to use?

- First of all, don't be daunted by the amount of choice you have. With trial and error, you can find what devices and apps suit you.

- Plan ahead. Decide which digital device and apps you are going to use ahead of your lecture.

- Don't be afraid to mix things up. You might want the best of both worlds and use a combination of traditional notebooks alongside some of your apps or devices. Experiment with what works for you.

- Take care of the technical details. Think about the length of the lecture. Will you have enough battery life in your devices or do you need to find plug sockets?

- Retain the lessons. If you are creating revision notes, what will help you to remember the ideas and concepts? Perhaps recording your notes and listening to them while you are doing other things. Or creating and highlighting text and images that you can access across multiple devices to aid your revision.

- Retrieve the lessons. Going digital makes it easy to retrieve information and notes. When writing your notes, use key words and tags to help you search for and retrieve information easily.

A student told us

'I get too distracted using my laptop to take notes.'

Beware of digital distractions! If you are using a laptop or tablet to take notes, and you have access to the internet, it is easy to get distracted by social media channels and chatting with friends online. Close down your social apps in lectures and focus.

Exploring the potential of digital tools

Today, it is easy to take our digital devices for granted, and we don't often access their full capabilities.

- Think about the digital devices and apps you already have. How can these be used to aid your learning and make student life easier for you?

- What apps do you already have on your phone or tablet that you can use to take notes?

- Explore what other apps are available.

'Master digital tools; don't let them master you.'

Congratulations

You have learned why to note-take and what good notes are like. Now we turn to the specifics of how to take them.

You can choose which methods suit you.

What is the outline method of note-taking?

10 second summary

The popular outline method of note-taking is easy to use and produces well-organized notes by making use of indentations and headings. It will help you to pick out the essential concepts and issues.

60 second summary

The outline method

The outline method is one of the most popular methods because you are organizing your notes as you go This saves time when you redo them. They are already, to some extent, organized. However, it is less easy to use with material which is disorganized in its presentation or which contains many formulas and charts.

In essence, it uses indentations and headings for the main topics and their subtopics. Indentations and headings highlight the importance of the key concepts and issues in the lecture or book from which the notes are being made.

Method choices

Everyone has different preferences about which note-taking methods to use. You may be influenced by the context of the note-taking (lecture or book for example). You may also be influenced by your learning styles or strengths and weaknesses. Whatever method you use, you can tweak it to suit your own needs.

How the outline method works

1 You write the main topic on the far left of the page and indent its subtopic and then the supporting points. You come back to the left for the next main topic.

2 The main topic means the subject of that part of the lecture or book.

3 The subtopic is an important aspect of the main topic.

4 The supporting points are facts or arguments or examples that relate to and support the subject or subtopic.

The outline method of note-taking

You start with the main topic and indent in order of importance.

A popular method producing organized notes.

A student told us

'Trying to indent while listening to my lecture got me in a muddle!'

Don't worry, a prepared layout page will help (Section 5) or you can organize your notes as you take them with headings, bullet points and numbering – don't try to indent.

Advantages of the outline method

- It is useful for taking notes on relatively well-structured lectures, articles, and books.

- It highlights the key points.

- It shows the relative importance of concepts and issues within the material.

- It gives shape and structure to your notes.

    Structure A framework, a whole arranged into parts.

- Because it is easy to use, it allows you to keep up with the pace of a lecture.

- It cuts down on the editing time when you redo your notes.

Disadvantages of the outline method

- It is not always suitable for subjects like science or maths, which include a substantial proportion of formulas and charts.

Chart A table or diagram setting out information.

- It doesn't work as well for lectures or books which are not well structured but jump about from idea to idea and back again.

Reviewing the outline method

How does the outline method of note-taking save time when you redo your notes?

....

....

With what kind of material is the outline method less easy to use?

....

....

How does the outline method highlight the most important points in the material?

....

....

Write down one of your own ideas about the online method.

....

....

ACTIVITY How to try out the outline method

Listen to a lecture. This could be at university, or a local talk on any subject, or listen to a TED talk. If you prefer, choose a lecture on the radio or television.

As you listen, use the outline method of note-taking.

....

....

....

....

....

....

....

....

....

....

....

....

....

....

....

Now ask yourself:

- ☐ Did I find it easy to take notes using the outline method as I listened?

- ☐ Do my notes follow the outline pattern: topic, subtopic, supporting material?

- ☐ Did I find it reasonably congenial to use this method?

- ☐ Do my notes capture most of the topics covered by the talk?

- ☐ Are my notes clear?

- ☐ Are my notes succinct but inclusive of the main points?

- ☐ Will my notes make a useful aide-mémoire for later use?

- ☐ Are my notes easy to edit: amend, add to, clarify, prune, etc.?

What do you think? Is this the right method of note-taking for you?

> 'Like a skeleton, an outline reveals the structure on which it all hangs!'

What is the Cornell method of note-taking?

10 second summary

The Cornell method of note-taking uses a particular page layout to help you take notes and also to include the title and date, your own ideas, and a summary.

60 second summary

Cornell: A notable method!

The Cornell method of note-taking is an inclusive method in that it ensures that you include, as well as the actual notes, the title and date of the notes, your own ideas about them, and a summary. Inclusive notes are particularly useful for helping you with your assignments and examination revision. This method can be used whether you are taking notes on a lecture or making notes on a book or article. It has many advantages and relatively few disadvantages. The Cornell method uses a sensible and easy page layout.

What is the page layout method of note-taking?

With the page layout approach you prepare the pages before taking your notes. Each layout method, including the Cornell and charting methods, divides the pages in its own unique way.

Cornell layout: Dividing the page

With the Cornell method, each page of notes is divided into four sections. A narrow section along the top is for the title and date. The centre section of the page is divided into two parts, about one third and two thirds of the space respectively, for your own ideas and for your actual notes. A slightly wider section along the bottom of the page is for the summary.

Title and date	
Own comments	Notes
Summary	

Because the pages are divided into four sections you will always record the title and date, your own ideas and a summary – as well as the actual notes. Without this page layout, simply taking notes, you could easily forget to include the topic or date, or some comments and questions of your own – all material which will be helpful to you when writing an assignment or doing examination revision.

This inclusive layout can be useful whether you are taking notes on a lecture or making notes on a book or an article. If you are making notes on a book, in the title section of the page you should record the author, the title of the book, the publisher and place of publication. If you are making notes on an article you will also need to record details of the book or journal which contains the article.

- This method uses a sensible and easy division of the page.

- Have several layout pages pre-prepared.

- Use more than one of these pages as required.

- Write your notes clearly. To redo them, simply add in your own comments and the summary.

- Having the column for your own comments alongside the notes column prompts you to think of questions and ideas of your own arising from the topic or prompted by the notes column.

Doing your summary

Doing a summary will develop your skills of picking out the important material. A good summary will also be useful when reviewing your notes for an assignment or exam revision. In the Cornell page layout the summary slot is smaller than the slot for your notes. This should prompt you to do a shortened version for your summary which simply gives a brief overview of the notes.

If you are making notes on an article, this will often have an abstract giving a brief overview. This will help you to do your summary.

An example of using the Cornell method on a lecture about learning styles

Learning Styles 5th November 2018	
Own comments	Notes
Is this plausible?	Significance controversial. No conclusive research.
Differing accounts cast doubt on the theory.	• The learning styles idea is that students learn more easily from material that is presented in a way that suits their particular LS • Diff numbers of LS identified: Verbal (text), Aural (heard); Visual (maps, diagrams); Kinaesthetic (interactive)
Teachers should use different approaches in a lesson anyway to offset boredom.	Imp question – what are the implications for the teacher?

Summary

It is claimed that learning styles vary and that this is significant in education. However, this is disputed and there is no compelling research. Commonly four learning styles are identified (verbal, visual, oral, kinaesthetic) and several more learning styles have been postulated. An important question: what, if any, are the implications of learning styles for our teaching?

Kinaesthetic learning Learning through the movement of your body or through your sense of touch.

Advantages of the Cornell method

- Works well for making notes on well-presented material.

- Easy to use.

- Encourages you to record the key points.

- Saves you time in redoing your notes. (It may be sufficient to simply amend your draft page.)

- Includes a summary, which is useful for exam revision.

- The left-hand column encourages you to reflect on the recorded material. This will encourage critical thinking and stimulate your ideas.

> **Critical thinking** Thinking which questions, assesses, judges, gives deeper consideration and thus does not simply accept that which is being claimed unreflectively.

- If you are taking notes digitally, you can either prepare a template document yourself, in Microsoft Word or Google Docs, or find templates online and then use these an infinite number of times.

Disadvantages of the Cornell method

- It is not suitable for all books or even all lectures. It will not work so well with disorganized material or material using a substantial number of formulas or charts.

- Several layout pages must be prepared before the lecture.

A student told us

'I always forget to prepare the pages before my lecture.'

It only takes a few seconds; you could make the sections while the class is settling down.

Before, during, and after

Before the lecture, prepare your pages. During it, record all the important information in a clear and organized way. After the lecture, include ideas and questions of your own, do the summary, and amend or redo your first draft notes.

Similarly, before reading a book prepare your pages and get a sense of the book from the preface and contents list. Whilst reading it, record all the important information and your own ideas and questions. After reading the book do the summary and amend your first draft notes if necessary.

Preface An introductory piece at the beginning of the book. This may be in addition to the Introduction to the book.

CHECK POINT Reviewing the Cornell method

How is the Cornell method of note-taking an inclusive method?

....

....

How can the Cornell method stimulate your own ideas?

....

....

What skill will writing a summary help you to develop?

....

....

Give two advantages of the Cornell method.

....

....

Give two disadvantages of the Cornell method.

....

....

'Be Prepared.'

ACTIVITY How to use Cornell

Prepare a Cornell page layout. Now make notes on one of the sections of this book using the page layout you have prepared.

What is the charting method of note-taking?

10 second summary

With the charting method, you construct a chart and create the number of columns that you will need. It is a useful method for recording detailed facts, statistics, or categorized data.

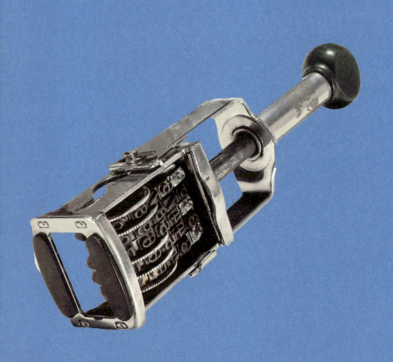

60 second
summary

Charts used for note-taking

There are many kinds of charts but the one used for note-taking is a division of the page into vertical columns. Simply rule down the page to create these. The number of columns depends on the information to be recorded.

Name the chart to show the subject. Label the columns to show aspects of the subject. The labels should reflect the type of information to be recorded in each column. Horizontal lines can be drawn across the page. This is often helpful in comparing subcategories.

Thus a chart is a visual record of substantial data which can be split into groups and gives ready comparisons between these groups by reading down and across the page. . Statistical data is often presented in chart form.

More about charts

- Charts can help you to remember a mass of detailed information.

- After you have taken your initial notes, sometimes you may find it possible to redo these as a chart.

- In an assignment, you may find it useful to present substantial data in chart form.

- Charts can be helpful when you do your examination revision.

Example of a column chart

Example of a column chart with horizontal sections

Example of a completed chart

Types of note-taking	Characteristics	Context	Pros	Cons
Outline	Indent and headings to organize	Lecture	Prioritizes	Not for disorganized material
Cornell	4-fold division of the page	Lectures and books	Encourages own comments and summary	Not for disorganized material
Charting	Chart format	Heavy data/ statistics	Conveys substantial data	For detailed information

Statistics Numbers and facts set out in order; organized to give detailed and comparative information.

A student told us

'I know it sounds silly, but I've never really known what a category is.'

A category is a class or group. The class or group have something in common which separates them from the things which are not in that class or group.

Advantages of the charting method

- Detailed or heavy information can be noted in a concise way.

- It is easier to absorb detailed information presented in this way.

- It is a useful way to redo some first draft notes.

- Such charts can be very useful in revising for examinations.

Disadvantages of the charting method

- It is a time-consuming way of redoing your notes (but, for some material, this time might be well worth investing).

- It is not possible to produce a chart for material which cannot be organized into categories of items which are subgroups of an overall subject.

CHECK POINT Comparing the outline, Cornell, and charting methods

Answer the following questions and compare your answers with the sample answers.

1   Write down two things that the outline and the Cornell methods have in common.

....

....

2   Write down one thing that the Cornell and charting methods have in common and one thing that is different.

....

....

3   Write down which of these three methods most appeals to you. Give a reason.

....

....

4   Give a reason why two other students might each prefer one of the other two methods.

....

....

CHECK POINT

Sample answers

1   They both involve organizing as you go. Neither works well for
    disorganized material.

2   They are both page layout methods. Charting does
    not include a summary.

3   Cornell – because this stimulates my own ideas and
    the page can simply be added to or amended to 'redo'.

4   Outline – no prior page preparation needed. Charting –
    loads of information and brilliant for revision.

 **Make a chart**

A chart can help you to organize your time as well as your notes.

Most of us can feel overwhelmed sometimes with everything we need to get done. Make a to-do list. Put this as the heading of the first column of your chart, with deadline, time needed, when to do, priority rating (high/low) in the following columns.

To-do list	Deadline	Time needed	When to do	Priority rating (high/low)

'Notes are your charter for success!'

What are the visual methods of note-taking?

10 second summary

Visual note-taking methods use structures (mind maps and spider diagrams), images, and organizers or connectors to capture and present information graphically without being text heavy.

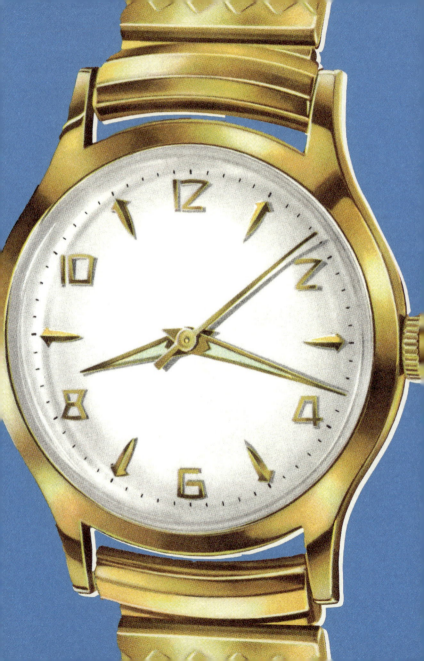

More about visual methods

Visual methods of note-taking, sometimes also called sketch-noting, make good use of colours, patterns, shapes, connectors, doodles, and images to create graphical representations of the information being learned. Visual note-taking uses a free-form rather than a linear style of capturing concepts and ideas and is often used for brainstorming sessions. Although this is a free-form and creative way of working, visual note-taking still gives you structure and process so that you can organize your notes, ideas, and concepts.

The captured information can be seen 'at a glance' and helps you to remember and retain the information.

Examples of visual note-taking

- Mind maps – a visual representation of a topic with the main idea at the centre of the page and associated ideas branching out.

- Spider diagrams – a type of mind map (they are called this because they resemble webs).

- Concept maps – this is similar in presentation to a mind map but goes further and highlights the links and relationships between topics.

- Bullet journals – a planning method that is a succinct and visual way of capturing information in a highly organized way.

- Flow charts – a chart that uses shapes in linear and logical paths to show the different potential outcomes or choices.

All these visual methods of note-taking use the same principles of a mind map. They have central ideas or topics which are then branched out in some way to capture the information. They are often on one page and you can see at a glance the concepts, links, and relationships.

An example of a mind map

There are different ways of creating mind maps. Simply draw them by hand or use one of the many mind mapping tools available free online. Or you can create your own using digital drawing or paint tools available from Microsoft or Apple's iTunes.

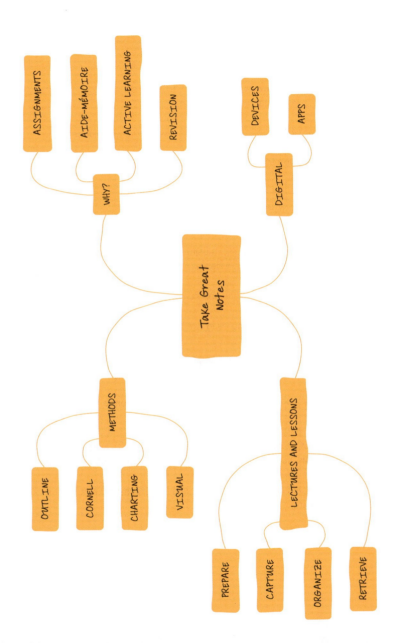

Advantages of visual notes

- They clearly show the relationships, hierarchies, and connections between individual pieces of information.

- They provide an overview of the topic or lecture at a glance.

- They help you to spot trends, patterns, and potential gaps in information.

- They encourage you to focus on the key points of a lecture or key points for revising.

- They provide mental triggers using images and graphics that will help you to remember concepts more easily.

- They are free-form in style and can be more fun and creative.

- You can create visual notes in written or digital format.

Disadvantages of visual note-taking

- You can become distracted creating the visual forms rather than focusing on the information.

- Visual formats are not for everyone. If you prefer to write notes in a linear way, you might be better choosing one of the other methods.

- Visual notes are generally not as detailed as some other forms of note-taking.

A student told us

'I haven't used visual note-taking before; I might not be any good at it.'

Visual note-taking doesn't need to be complicated. Start off by using simple shapes, and just one or two colours. Experiment with more colours and shapes as you develop your visual note-taking skills.

Overcoming roadblocks

I can't draw well enough or fast enough	You don't need expert drawing skills. Just decide on your layout, keep it simple and develop your skills with practice.
I'm not creative	Anyone can be creative. You just need to develop your skills. Experiment with different layouts, fonts, colours, and shapes. Practise and improve.
I don't know where to put ideas on the page	Start with your main topic heading at the centre of the page and branch out from there. Experiment with shapes and connectors.
I don't want to run out of room on the page	Think about your layout before you start. How much text will you use? What shapes will you use? How many ideas and subcategories will you capture?

CHECK POINT Reviewing contexts and methods for visual note-taking

Visual methods of note-taking can be used in a variety of ways and settings. Make a list of the different situations where you can use visual note-taking and the methods you can use.

....

....

....

....

....

....

....

....

....

....

....

....

....

....

....

....

ACTIVITY | Create your own mind map or spider diagram

1 Take a large sheet of paper – A3 and A2 sizes work well depending on whether you are capturing a lecture or writing up notes for revision.

2 Draw a circle in the middle of the page and in this write your main topic heading.

3 Create subtopics by branching off from the main subject.

4 Make it fun by choosing a topic you know very little about and brainstorm the knowledge you have. You will be surprised at what you do know.

5 Try also using a digital mind map or spider diagram. Look for free versions online.

'A picture is worth a thousand words.'

What are the electronic methods of note-taking?

10 second summary

Electronic note-taking captures information using digital devices including laptops, tablets, mobile phones, audio, and video recorders. A variety of apps can be used on these devices to support note-taking.

Enhance your note-taking

Capturing information and being able to store and retrieve it effectively is the key to taking great notes. You can make this a lot more powerful by getting creative with the tools you use. Most students these days will have multiple digital devices yet don't use them to their full capacity. Think about how you can use photos and videos to enhance your notes using your mobile phone apps. Capture website links and articles using note-taking apps to help with your research. Do quick searches on the Internet while in lectures if there's a particular point or idea that you want more information on immediately. (But remember not to get too distracted while online!).

A student told us

'There are so many new technologies. It's difficult to know which ones will best help me.'

It can be daunting. The digital world is rapidly changing all the time and it's hard to keep pace. Assess what you already have available to you. Also try searching on Google or YouTube for advice and tips. Select one or two that appeal to you the most and then try them out.

Choosing your digital toolkit

Digital devices, tools, programs, apps, and websites open up a whole new world of possibilities for note-taking. They can increase your productivity, give you freedom, and allow you to have flexibility.

Using a laptop or mobile device in lectures will allow you to capture information and ideas that you can than organize and store easily.

With mobile devices, such as phones and tablets, you have the freedom to revise wherever you want – on the bus, during your lunch break, in the library, or during group sessions. Because these devices are small and portable, you don't have to carry around heavier items such as books and laptops.

Devices

- Mobile phones – enable you to access your information and material on the go.

- Tablets – can be used to create, record, capture, store, and retrieve information, lecture notes, revision notes, etc.

- Laptops – will be used for storing and organizing your lecture notes and research information.

- Audio and video recording devices – use your mobile phone or tablet or devices that are designed for this purpose.

Applications and programs

Applications are computer programs, often referred to as apps. There are new apps and programs being developed all the time as technology advances, which makes note-taking on digital devices so much easier and also fun. They allow you to import PDFs, images and charts, audio files, video files, and even whole book texts. This means that you can organize the information in ways that will help you to remember the information and be more productive when it comes to revising the information and applying the lessons learned.

- Word processing programs such as Microsoft Word, Google Docs, LibreOffice, or Apache Office.

- Note-taking applications such as Microsoft OneNote, Evernote or Goodnotes.

- Some digital notebooks such as Moleskin also have applications so that you can upload your notes electronically and synchronise (sync) these across multiple devices.

Digital handwritten notes

There are a growing number of apps that allow you to make 'handwritten' notes on digital devices, and the technology is improving all the time so that this method feels like writing on notepaper. There are even 'paper' notebooks that have embedded technology so that you can upload your notes electronically to your laptop or to a cloud-based platform which will allow you to access your notes easily across multiple devices later. This gives you the best of both worlds.

Digital note-taking goes further than handwritten text. With note-taking apps you can import images, PDFs, articles, and even books. The technology allows you to annotate and then combine these with your text, charts, doodles and mind maps. From there you can then create your own PDFs, which you can print out and place in revision folders or place on a wall as visual aids when revising.

List the digital devices, apps, and programmes that you have access to and evaluate how they can help you to take great notes.

What is available at your university?

....

....

....

....

....

....

....

How does your university use digital technology to make your life as a student easier?

....

....

....

....

....

....

....

ACTIVITY Experiment with devices

Using a laptop

Choose a note-taking method as outlined in the sections above and set up a template of one or several of these in a word processing programme. Test this method by taking notes of a news programme or documentary. Evaluate the effectiveness of this method.

Using a tablet

If you are fortunate enough to have the latest iPad Pro, Microsoft Surface Pro, or Samsung Galaxy Tab and special pencil and you would like to try digital written notes, then select an app such as GoodNotes to help with this.

Enhancing your note-taking

Experiment with the audio or video recording facilities on your mobile device.

'Digital tools open up a whole new world.'

Congratulations

You have now learned about several methods of note-taking.

Think about which you like and why.

How do I take notes in a lecture?

10 second
summary

Capturing concepts and ideas from lectures requires preparation and making good use of the tools and processes best suited to your learning preferences and the task at hand.

60 second summary

Note-taking in lectures: it's all about quality not quantity

Taking notes in lectures means having to listen to and capture a lot of information, as well as trying to understand the concepts and ideas at the same time. It's easy to fall into the trap of trying to take notes verbatim so that you capture everything, but this isn't necessary. What you need to aim for is taking notes that will aid your learning. With good planning and preparation, you can take notes in lectures effectively and then use processes and systems that will enable you to organize, store, and retrieve them easily and efficiently.

Planning and preparation

You will now have the tools you need to take great notes, whether you are using more traditional methods or you are going digital. But a little further planning and preparation will make life a lot easier and save you time and effort.

There are three main elements to taking notes on lectures: capturing the information, organizing it efficiently, and retrieving it effectively.

What you need to consider

1   The type of lecture and how it will be presented. Will there be slides? Will the lecture be recorded on video? How many students will attend? How long will the lecture last? Will it be presenting detailed information or ideas and concepts? Will you be expected to participate?

2   The venue – is the room small or large? How will it be laid out? Is there access to plug sockets? What is the lighting like? Will there be desks or will the lecture be held in a theatre?

3   Having considered the type of lecture and the venue, what note-taking tools would be the best to use?

The key elements

During any period of study where you are attending lots of lectures and participating in group study sessions, you will very quickly amass a lot of material. This will include your notes, but you will also need to link these to the resources and other materials on the topics you are studying. The time you will spend in planning and organizing your note-taking and course materials will be time that is well invested and, far from being a chore, it will give you more freedom and flexibility and make you more productive in your studies.

Capture

Taking notes in lectures is all about capturing ideas, concepts, and information and doing this in the most efficient ways. You will want to record the lecture so that you can apply the lessons learned either in your exams or when you are giving group presentations.

Actively listen

Try to avoid the urge to take the notes verbatim. Instead, try to comprehend the overall messages or lessons and capture these using the note-taking methods you prefer to use. Remember to:

- Emphasize key words and concepts.

- Highlight notes that will require further attention later.

Avoid distractions

If you are taking notes electronically using a laptop or tablet, avoid going on to your social media channels or looking at your email inbox. Remember to:

- Focus on the lecture and what you are trying to learn.

- Switch off notifications on your apps or close them.

Use the right tools

We have discussed numerous methods and tools for note-taking in this book. Choose the right ones for the lecture and use them effectively. Remember to:

- Use your note-taking templates if you have these.

- Make sure you have enough battery power if you are using recording devices.

Organize

Choose a system for organizing your notes that suits your style of working. Some people are more organized than others, and some people find filing a chore and a headache. Your system doesn't have to be complicated. It just needs to allow you to retrieve information efficiently and when you need it.

- Use separate files or folders for each subject.

- Use file dividers where appropriate.

- Label files and folders clearly.

- Number and label files and pages so you can retrieve them easily.

- If storing notes electronically, use relevant key words and tags.

Retrieve

If you spend time searching for notes that you haven't organized properly, you will end up getting frustrated. A few simple techniques using tags and key words or filing your physical notes using a well-thought-out system will save you a lot of time and effort.

- Keep a note of key words and search terms and tags to help you retrieve your notes easily. Some key words and phrases will be obvious.

- Refresh your memory on the key aspects of your filing system. If you have difficulty retrieving notes at any time, either improve or simplify your system.

- Remember to return your notes to their correct folders, or if you are working electronically remember to save the most recent version.

- Take regular backups of any electronic systems. Don't keep your notes on one memory stick. Your notes are too valuable to lose.

A student told us

'I am not very organized and I spend ages looking for information I have filed away.'

Develop good habits when taking notes and have a good system in place that will make it much easier to file away as soon as your lecture has ended.

Making your note-taking more effective

Good note-taking in lectures is about more than simply capturing the information. Think about the key elements needed to make note-taking more effective. Which of these elements can you improve on?

....

....

....

ACTIVITY Active listening and note-taking

- Practise active listening by taking notes of a news broadcast or documentary on the television or radio.

- Experiment with one or two different methods of note-taking.

- After you have taken the notes, write a short summary outlining what the broadcast or document item was about.

....

....

....

....

....

....

....

....

....

....

- Play back the news broadcast or documentary later.

  ❑ Did you capture the information?

  ❑ Did you understand the key messages being conveyed?

- Are there are any areas where you could improve your active listening and note-taking?

....

....

....

'Avoid frustration by planning properly and being organized.'

How do I take notes on an article or book?

10 second summary

To grasp the subject of a book, check the contents and preface before reading it and taking notes. Before taking notes on an article, ensure you understand any technical vocabulary.

60 second summary

Note-taking from a text

You need to have notes on all the relevant books and articles that you have read during your studies. You need a concise record of the important concepts, research findings, arguments, theories, and influential thinkers in these texts. Think critically as you read; this will stimulate your own ideas. Record these ideas too.

You will need to be able to readily find these important concepts, research findings, etc. for your assignments. To do this, ensure that your notes from all the relevant books and articles are well organized, separated and distinguished from one from another, well labeled, and well stored.

Note-taking as you read

Books

Before you take notes on a book, get a sense of the author's viewpoint, from the contents list, preface, and blurb on the back. Notice the contents of the different chapters because only some of them may be relevant. Don't attempt to make notes on the whole book in one go. Make notes chapter by chapter, or even do sections of a chapter. You do not need to note what you already know or to note irrelevant chapters.

Chapters

Sometimes only one chapter of a book will be relevant to your assignment, but it may be a very useful one. Simply take notes on this one chapter. Remember to keep a record of the details of the book it is from (author, date, publisher, place of publication) and the chapter title and page numbers.

Articles

Articles are sometimes complicated. They are often written for academics. You may need to read an article two or three times and to check the technical vocabulary before reading to take notes. Nevertheless, being much shorter than books they take less time to read. And, being much shorter, articles are more focused on a topic compared to books. An article which is focused on the topic of your assignment may be very useful, but don't forget to reference it!

Technical vocabulary
Words relating to a particular discipline and understood in the same way by those trained in that discipline.

Taking notes on a book, a chapter, or an article

- Record key facts, key concepts, central theories, important arguments, and influential thinkers.

- Also record your own responses: your ideas, arguments, reasons, and questions.

A student told us

'I just know I won't have time to read all the books and articles on the recommended reading list.'

Learn to be selective in what you read, but do read as much as you reasonably can.

Being selective

To start with, focus on what you need to read for your assignments.

- Read introductory texts first to get a sense of your studies.

- Read the books and articles that your tutor draws attention to.

- Choose books which are inviting to read – because they include chapter summaries for example.

'I don't understand what my lecturer means by "think critically."'

Ask questions. Do I agree with this? Does he give me a good reason or some evidence? Is he making a reasonable assumption? Is there an alternative point of view?

Using books and articles

Try not to be in awe of the books and articles recommended to you. Don't forget to be critical. The author is not always right! As we said above, don't flounder in an ocean of reading. Be selective. However, it will be boring for your tutor to read the same things in everyone's assignment. If, in addition to the recommended reading, you can find time to read a little outside of this, you may bring a fresh perspective, a touch of originally to your work.

Try to own core books and photocopy significant articles. This allows you to mark the text.

- Circle key words.

- Underline possible quotes.

- Draw a line by the side of important concepts, theories, arguments, and thinkers.

- Put a star by useful definitions.

Don't forget to note the pages of these marked passages at the front of your notes.

Your books are your tools. Don't be afraid to write in them.

Top tips

1 Start on a new page for each new chapter.

2 Always include a summary.

3 Use a page layout, such as Cornell, if you find this helpful.

4 When you redo your notes, try to make them as concise as possible, without missing out essentials.

5 Think about how you store these notes so that you can find them very easily. For example, you could redo the notes on cards to be stored in a box file in alphabetical order by author, or you could store your notes using an electronic system.

Active reading

Practise being an active reader by reading with a task in mind. For example, now you have finished reading this book, reread it and make notes on the 10 things which you have found most useful.

1 ....

2 ....

3 ....

4 ....

5 ....

6 ....

7 ....

8 ....

9 ....

10 ....

Practising how to mark a text

Go through this book and mark the text. Circle key words, underline key sentences, draw a line by significant passages, put a star by useful definitions, and add your own responsive thoughts and questions.

'Reading is knowledge and knowledge is power.'

FINAL CHECK POINT How to know you are done

Do you understand how note-taking will help you with assignments, examination revision, and the skills of selecting and organizing key material? ❏

Can you give at least five characteristics of good notes? ❏

What digital tools do you already have to help you take great notes? ❏

How does the outline method of note-taking help you to prioritize your material? ❏

Can you mark out a Cornell page layout and identify three ways in which using this layout can be helpful to you as a student? ❏

Can you describe the kind of material which charts are
useful for presenting? ❏

Can you name two advantages and two disadvantages of visual
note-taking methods? ❏

How do electronic methods of note-taking give you freedom? ❏

Why is it not effective to take notes verbatim in lectures? ❏

Can you give useful advice for note-taking from:

A] books? ❏

B] chapters in books? ❏

C] articles? ❏

Glossary

Academic   Learned, theoretical, of the University. An academic is a university teacher.

Aide-mémoire   Something to help you remember, a reminder.

App   An application that can be downloaded to a mobile device or computer.

Chart   A table or diagram setting out information.

Concept   An idea, often a general or abstract idea.

Critical thinking   Thinking which questions, assesses, judges, gives deeper consideration and thus does not simply accept that which is being claimed unreflectively.

Digital   Methods of recording or storing information electronically.

Organize   Arrange and form into a logical sequence.

Preface   An introductory piece at the beginning of the book. This may be in addition to the Introduction to the book.

Statistics   Numbers and facts set out in order; organized to give detailed and comparative information.

Structure   A framework, a whole arranged into parts.

Summary   A shortened form of a piece giving only the main points.

Further reading and resources

Books

Buzan, T. (2011) *Buzan's Study Skills: Mind Maps, Memory Techniques, Speed Reading and More! (Mind Set)*. Harlow: BBC Active/Pearson.

Godfrey. J. (2010) *Reading and Making Notes*. Basingstoke: Palgrave MacMillan.

Leicester, M., Taylor, D. (2017) *Get a Better Grade: Seven Steps to Excellent Essays and Assignments*. London: SAGE.

Online resources

Mariana's Study Corner: www.youtube.com/channel/UCEHp_b02l0GvTYCBPX_0w1g

Digital note-taking using OneNote: www.youtube.com/watch?v=MBwU7labwKE&t=0s&list=PLl1eBogZ8n7JyrrhqBSkwM5_tjJseNDdg&index=4